FOCUS

— ON —

TODAY

HOW LIVING IN THE PRESENT CAN TRANSFORM YOUR FUTURE

JOHN MARTIN

Published and Distributed by
SOUND WISDOM
PO Box 310
Shippensburg, PA 17257-0310
717-530-2122
info@soundwisdom.com
www.soundwisdom.com

While efforts have been made to verify information contained in this publication, neither the author nor the publisher assumes any responsibility for errors, inaccuracies, or omissions. While this publication is chock-full of useful, practical information, it is not intended to be legal or accounting advice. All readers are advised to seek competent lawyers and accountants to follow laws and regulations that may apply to specific situations. The reader of this publication assumes responsibility for the use of the information. The author and publisher assume no responsibility or liability whatsoever on the behalf of the reader of this publication.

ISBN 13 TP: 978-1-64095-421-2
ISBN 13 eBook: 978-1-64095-422-9

For Worldwide Distribution, Printed in the U.S.A.
1 2 3 4 5 6 /25 24 23 22

Other Sound Wisdom titles by John Martin

Empower Yourself
Increase Your Personal Productivity
Choose Your Perspective
Focused and Free

Do not wait for a change of environment before you act; get a change of environment by action. You can so act upon the environment in which you are now as to cause yourself to be transferred to a better environment. Hold with faith and purpose the vision of yourself in the better environment, but act upon your present environment with all your heart, and with all your strength, and with all your mind.

—WALLACE D. WATTLES

CONTENTS

AUTHOR'S NOTE

Just a couple days ago, I was working on a book about becoming free—financially, mentally, emotionally—through sharp focus and effective daily habits. I tried and tried to finish the book. For a year, I had been struggling with it.

Some invisible force was preventing me from sitting down and typing the information that I had learned and believed would also help the reader.

As the deadlines blew by, a fear crept into my mind suggesting that I was failing—I did not know what I was writing about or maybe I had nothing worth sharing after all. The self-doubt grew. Perhaps I was not in line with my calling and purpose.

All this culminated in crippling anxiety and a lack of productivity. I was distracted and trapped, not *focused and free* like the book was titled (now available from your favorite online bookseller). And so...

One morning, I was searching for ideas, motivation, a voice from the sky to give me some sort of inspiration to get the words flowing again. Looking through some old journals, I found an entry from exactly one year ago and within was a line that read *"Focus on TODAY."*

It hit me.

The problem was I was worried and thinking about almost everything outside of today and the current moment. Projecting myself into the future clouded my mind. After this realization, my mind was flooded with insights and the powerful potential of recognizing when you stray from the present and being able to come back to it.

I wrote like a maniac and finished the book.

This was my personal experience, and this same idea of staying present could help you in your own life. Not only immediately as it had just helped me, but the far-reaching impacts of living this way every day could change the trajectory of your future!

Anyone one who wants to grow their business, improve their body, anyone who wants to improve their relationships, networking skills, financial position—the principles and skills that could be gained from living in the present each day are innumerable!

INTRODUCTION

...Or how to use the present moment to accomplish your goals

The idea that our present moments determine our future moments is a big picture look at this transformation, but I want to offer you the tips and tricks that will help you come back to the present moment when you are full of anxious thoughts about what might happen tomorrow or about other people's opinions.

The ways in which living in the present moment can impact and transform your future are many. Mindfulness, which is defined broadly as the state of being conscious or aware of the present moment while acknowledging and accepting one's thoughts, feelings, and bodily sensations (definition from Oxford languages), brings increased concentration, confidence, productivity, and perseverance.

Aside from all the above-mentioned benefits, being present necessarily reduces anxiety which leads to better overall health and well-being.

Would any of these qualities be of improvement to your life?

Once you understand the possibilities and peace that can come from living in the here and now, you will want to live in that place more often. It begins with realizing and experiencing being present in the moment.

What so many of us fail to see or we tend to forget is that each minute of each day makes up our years alive. And as fast as your minutes go by, that is how fast your life sails by. It is a good truth to remember as needed.

What you do with your minutes makes up the story of your life.

From the here and now, you can manifest your future through the imagination. When you exclude the external reality of stress and worry, you are free to imagine possibilities. You are free to imagine becoming what you've always been drawn toward in the back of your mind. That nagging little voice you have dismissed over a lifetime of making the practical choice, becomes foremost in your mind as you experience the here and now.

The more you overcome your impulses to quit, your internal excuses telling you to resume your old habits, the more joy and rewards you will experience. Until one day, after many successes, you will find that the thrill of victory comes from the actual work itself rather than the results.

No one will do the work for you, so do not compare yourself to others. Do not go on this journey with others. It is your life and yours alone to live and grow within. There are all kinds of people you can think of that do it better than you, that have stronger willpower than you, or so it would seem. None of that matters. All that matters is that you hold on to the desire to grow and stay focused on today to get through your temptations and obstacles.

What you do with your minutes makes up the story of your life.

If you can manage to stay within the point of reality that is NOW, you will notice several awesome improvements in your life:

1. You will be more productive and less obsessive about time.
2. You will look forward to daily tasks as challenges.
3. You will stay calm and confident and patient in the face of stress.
4. You will rarely worry about what others are thinking of you.

And a bonus benefit is that you begin to get all the things you used to chase, only now without trying to attain them.

You begin sinking into flow state so often that it becomes commonplace.

That is the goal, flow state. To live in accordance with our purpose (being the best person we can be). We get away from our purpose when we allow too many thoughts to invade our mind. We allow too many thoughts to invade our mind when we are not focused on a task. We are not focused on a task when we make our goals and tasks too big and complicated.

When we are not present, we get into trouble. If we stay present, we stay engaged and busy achieving our purpose. Content and confident.

Do not be distracted by the nonsense because the nonsense is always present. Even when it is not around you externally, it will present itself in the form of thoughts in your imagination. Random daydreams, fantasies without reason. Bizarre thoughts. Memories.

Become too strong for the interference from outside and too engaged for the resistance from within. When you are able to master each moment, you have found the key to transforming your life.

Do all this by taking positive action right now. And again tomorrow. And the next day. Take pride in your consistency. Do what your conscience is calling you to do.

Immersed in the present, you are connected to the source.

Being present in the moment, you forget about the person you thought you were and become the person you want to be.

— 1 —

HERE AND NOW

That's what you always forget, isn't it?
I mean, you forget to pay attention to what's happening.
And that's the same as not being here and now.
—Aldous Huxley, *Island*

LESS THAN A YEAR before he died, famous writer Aldous Huxley's final book, *Island*, was published. The novel begins with Will Farnaby, one of the main characters in the story, shipwrecked on the island of Pala. Pala is a place where the people and their leaders have adopted a way of living that blends the best of eastern and western philosophy and technological advances. For example, they would use the technology of refrigeration, but not of television. They are selective in using advances in medicine and science, and resist adopting every aspect of the progress of advertising or industrialization. It is a group of people who value awareness.

Huxley presents this utopian society (contrasted with his dystopian society of *Brave New World*) that offers ideas on how problems of civilization could be solved or improved. One of the many unique features of the island are trained-to-talk myna birds which fly around often squawking mantras like "attention!" and "Here and now!" as a reminder to the islanders to pay attention to what was happening and not to be mentally distracted from the here and now.

So many of our problems come as a result of worrying and building anxiety about events that have not happened yet or things we cannot control. Other issues arise when we try to escape the here and now. When we try to avoid the problems and the work we need to do on ourselves by chasing pleasure and escapism, we create new problems in addition to finding ourselves in a cycle of negative energy that is easier to enter than to exit.

Let us unpack this idea of here and now..

The "here" is the physical space in which you find yourself reading this sentence. Are you sitting in a chair? Are you laying down on the couch? Are you walking down the hallway scanning the kindle version on your phone? Are you driving down the interstate listening to this audiobook while barely paying attention because you can't remember if you did that one thing for work or if you need to pick up anything at the grocery store? The "now" is literally the moment you are in right now. It is the seconds that it takes to read this sentence.

Wherever you are, you are here and now.

Our mental health can be improved by remembering this truth throughout the day—grounding ourselves when we start getting anxious thoughts. And it is incredible how many ways this way of living and thinking can help our businesses and our physical health as well. But first, let's explore a couple of ways to practice grounding ourselves in the moment on a daily basis.

JUST BREATHE

One effective way to come back to the moment and calm the body's physiological reaction to nervousness or overthinking is to breathe deeply and exhale slowly over a period of ten seconds or so. Take a deep breath, then exhale slowly. Repeat. Your body will become more restful and your mind will begin to quiet itself.

From this place you can move into an awareness of the here and now through physical sensations or observations.

PAY ATTENTION TO THE DETAILS OF THE MOMENT

As an exercise in coming back to present moments, try paying attention to the tiniest details of the current moment. What your hands are touching or how your feet are positioned on the floor or ground. How your back is resting or your neck and shoulders positioned. Listen to the sounds around you. Do you hear a dishwasher or drying machine, the AC unit or a fan?, or maybe the wind is blowing outside and a window in your house is rattling. All these little things are part of the present moment, and when you intentionally observe, listen, feel, smell, and or touch your immediate surroundings, it is a way of coming back to the here and now.

Repeating these practices whenever you can regardless of whether you are stressed, angry, or feeling perfectly calm is a good use of time and the repetition will help you to acquire the ability to deploy mindfulness when most needed.

This skill of grounding yourself in the present is valuable because it allows you—for the moment—to forget your worries, to forget your doubts, fears, and past failures. Coming back to the moment helps you to understand that this moment is all you have, and it is a brand-new starting point. You are alive and you recognize this truth. And it follows that if you are at least able to recognize and exist in the present moment, then you are able to keep trying to improve your situation no matter how dire it might be. It is a reset moment, an opportunity to begin again.

> *This moment is all you have, and it is a brand-new starting point.*

PRACTICE BEING PRESENT

After practice and time spent consistently existing in the present, you will find you are more honest with yourself and authentic in your interactions with others. This authenticity comes as a byproduct of ridding yourself of the bad habits and vices of escapism that cloud your judgment, exacerbate anxiety, and blind yourself to who you really are.

Finding contentment in the present moment, you are soon able to quit your vices because you begin to see more clearly the root of your problems and why you turned to the negative activities or substances in the first place.

The lack of discipline and baggage of coping mechanisms that comes from years of rationalizing bad habits and avoidance of the truth, and the eventual negative cycle that is established and so hard to break—if you can come to this lifestyle of focusing on now, today, just this moment, you can find your way out of the madness, frustration, and exhausting regret of failing to control your actions. One minute, one hour, one day at a time, you will find your way out.

When you first start on this journey of living in the present, you may be discouraged by your lack of ability to stay in the moment. You might find yourself drifting off in your mind to worries and anxious thoughts. This is understandable. We are programmed to worry after all, and many of us live in a culture that feeds fear and anxiety, not mindfulness and peace.

Be patient with yourself during these initial days and keep trying. Understand that if you are self-aware enough to be able to recognize when you are in the state of this cycle, your failures can be opportunities and you will be able to keep trying. In fact it is useful to look at your vices as opportunities to strengthen yourself through

Be patient with yourself on your journey of living in the present.

denying yourself the pleasure that you gain from them. In this way, you turn a weakness into a strength, and a failure into a chance to grow.

PERSONAL REFLECTIONS

Do you find yourself looking to escape the here and now? Do you notice what triggers the desire to escape?

What do you do when you find yourself distracted from what you need to be doing?

How patient are you with yourself? Do you talk negatively to yourself when you make a mistake?

In which areas of your life could you use more discipline?

What are some ways you can think of to bring yourself back to the present moment when your thoughts wander off?

What bad habits are you holding on to? Is it time to let them go?

Once again, can you pay attention to the sensory details of the place you are in and find yourself in this present moment of existence?

— 2 —

THE POWER OF JOURNALING

In the journal I do not just express myself more
openly than I could to any person; I create myself.
—Susan Sontag

AROUND SIX YEARS AGO, I started writing in a notebook and found it to be a great way to sort through the issues that I was thinking about.

I started carrying the notebook with me each day and writing my thoughts any chance I could get or whenever it was warranted. Sometimes just 30 seconds here or there is all it took to get something down. The notebooks I carried (and still carry) are maybe 3 × 4.5 inches in size and fit easily into the pocket of a pair of jeans or a shirt. As I write this book today based on words I wrote in one of those journals years ago, I would say that these past six years have become the most productive years of my life so far.

Find what works for you in terms of a notebook or journal, but keeping it with you and accessible is valuable in many ways. First, you can practice coming back to the present moment by taking out that notebook and writing when you find yourself distracted and having a difficult time concentrating.

The physical act of writing requires your attention to be fully on the act and the words that you are writing. Use that hack to write down what you should be doing at the moment and then return to the task at hand. This habit can be turned into a goal-setting technique where you write down not only what you should be doing now, but also what you will do next.

> *The physical act of writing requires your attention.*

Secondly, **journaling relieves tension and alleviates frustration.** When you get upset with the actions of another person, instead of firing off an angry response in person or via email or text, write that text or email in your notebook. Write all about the situation and your annoyance and get it all out on the pages so it takes up less space in your mind and notice as your frustration dissipates.

Make lists for the day. They could be work-related, personal, grocery lists, whatever the case, it is nice to have a list with you to help you stay focused and organized. I know many people use their phone for this purpose, but again, there is a certain refocusing that comes with getting out a pen and notebook and writing it down.

As you write down more and more information, you will start to see patterns emerge when you look back on your words. You will see the character of yourself on those pages. Your journals can become the blueprint for your own personal transformation. In writing down your thoughts, desires, and goals, you will begin outlining the path that is your calling in life.

Write down interesting quotes that you hear. Write down those creative ideas that come to you during an otherwise average day. Develop the habit of writing.

Mark Twain, Charles Darwin, Marie Curie, and Anne Frank are just a few people in history who changed the world and their work is in many ways attributable to the journals they kept.

Write, journal, scribble, and draw away. Let the anger and anxieties drift away. You never know when something you write down will be a source of inspiration to you or at the very least, an indication of how much you have grown from then until now.

Your journals become a history of your life and a valuable record of the human experience.

Start now: In the journaling section at the end of this book, write down some of your answers to these questions and the ones that follow the remaining chapters.

PERSONAL REFLECTIONS

What could you learn about yourself if you could go back in time and see your thoughts recorded?

When would be the best time for you to sit down and write out your thoughts?

What goals do you have that could be served by writing parts of them down each day?

What visions do you have that could be made more concrete through repeatedly journaling the details?

Can you imagine reducing your stress levels by journaling throughout the day?

Do you have a way of keeping a journal accessible as often as possible?

What time in your day are you most likely to come up with creative ideas?

If you already maintain the habit of journaling, where could you find time to journal more often?

In what ways could you use the practice of writing in your journal to come back to the present moment?

— 3 —
LET GO OF WORRIES

Worry does not empty tomorrow of its sorrow;
it empties today of its strength.
—Corrie Ten Boom

WE COULD ALL DO with a bit less worry, and if you can put yourself in the present moment right this second, you will probably realize there is no reason for immediate unease.

Of course, there are things that we are better off worrying about. If we fail to worry about paying the bills and neglect writing out the check to the electric company, or the trash company, we'll have bigger problems to worry about. But typically these are not the types of worries that plague us. It is usually things we have no control over.

Even if we do have control over them, there are steps we can take to reduce our anxious thoughts. Exercise is a big one. Taking a walk in the morning or a run or lifting weights will reduce the amount of cortisol in your body which causes stress. Exercise also increases the production of endorphins in your body which will in turn make you feel good.

With bills and appointments and these kinds of tasks, we can solve our uneasiness by being organized enough so that we are not late. Make a list, keep a monthly planner, automate as many bills through your bank account as you can.

But even organization is not always enough to prevent our active imagination from conjuring up more worries. What about all the anxious thoughts that pop into our heads throughout the day?

What will they think of me?

What should I say?

How do I look?

I'm not good enough.

I don't belong here.

How am I coming across right now?

Did they mean that as an insult?

Why did they not text/email back?

I need to get that report, presentation, or publication done.

Maybe I need to find a new job.

I need a haircut.

What should we do for dinner?

What if the stock market crashes?

If only I was rich.

If only my side business was more successful.

There are any number of variations of thoughts about money, potential tragedies, relationships ending, worries about children and money that arise and pass and before you know it, you have completely forgotten about what we are actually doing right this minute. your mind is lost in a rabbit-hole of concern and agitation.

Your constant introspection can become the obstacle to your peace.

Let go of all that is not now.

You have to come back to the moment and let go of all that is not now. This is the way to stop the endless chatter in your mind.

OVER-IDENTIFYING WITH THOUGHTS

Imagine not thinking.

Trying to imagine not thinking causes thoughts to arise.

We have to think about things. It is not as though we could exist without thinking for very long. We have to remember to pick up our child from school or to attend a meeting or to make a sales call.

But being able to go without thinking for a period of time, or to at least gain a perspective *outside* of our thoughts is useful and important to becoming a present-minded person. There are numerous books on this and one of the most instructive for me is Eckert Tolle's *The Power of Now*. What we are talking about are the negative thoughts, the nonsensical thoughts, the thoughts without basis or purpose that serve to delay us, cause us to doubt, and derail us from our calling in life.

THREE WAYS TO STOP OVERTHINKING

1. Acknowledge the random nature of thoughts
2. Breathe deeply and force yourself back to the present through physical sensation (touch the chair you are sitting on, do some form of exercise)
3. Write some of your thoughts down quickly

Daily, we are bombarded with thoughts that have nothing to do with what we are doing at the moment. Our thinking can be erratic. So if we can be the observer of those thoughts, we can decide which ones to be attentive to.

The goal of getting outside your mind is to recognize, for example, that just because you *think* that you are not good enough does not necessarily mean it is true that you are not.

It could be true, but such a thought deserves further examination and should not be taken at face value. If you let yourself get into the habit of believing all the thoughts you have about yourself, you could find yourself either overestimating or underestimating your abilities and these miscalculations could slow down the process of achieving your goals.

Observe and choose which thoughts you dwell upon.

You can observe and choose which thoughts you dwell upon, give credence to, or discard and push out of your mind altogether. This level of awareness will narrow and focus your intentionality when it comes to listening to the noise in your head and offer clarity in your decision-making, encourage positivity in your attitude, and strengthen your resolve.

WHY WORRY?

The same is true for the worrisome thoughts.

Worry is a state of mind based upon fear. It works slowly, but persistently. It is insidious and subtle. Step by step it "digs itself in" until it paralyzes one's reasoning faculty, destroys self-confidence and initiative. Worry is a form of sustained fear caused by indecision therefore it is a state of mind which can be controlled. —Napoleon Hill, Think and Grow Rich

I struggle with anxious thoughts; many people do. You may too. There is a story shared by Florence Scovel Shinn in her book, *The Game of Life and How to Play it*, about how a man was able to overcome his mostly irrational fears by simply reading a sign:

*A very brilliant man who has attained great success told me he had suddenly erased all fear from his consciousness by reading a sign which hung in a room. He saw printed in large letters this statement: "**Why worry? It will probably never happen.**" These words were stamped indelibly upon his subconscious mind, and he now has a firm conviction that only good can come into his life and, therefore, only good can manifest.*

As simplistic as it may seem, this story is a great example of the power of the subconscious mind and also the way in which we grant our surface-level thoughts and fears too much influence. Our goal is to move into a lifestyle where we control our thoughts rather than the other way around.

When we let negative thoughts take root in our mind, not only do we miss out on the moment we are in, we also allow the negativity to infect us in all other areas of our lives. It is a dark cloud that can follow us the rest of the day or longer if we let it.

Observing and controlling your thoughts is the name of the game and the key to letting go of that which worries us.

PERSONAL REFLECTIONS

What do you worry about most frequently?

Would you say you worry as a habit?

What areas of your life could be improved if you were able to let go of anxious thoughts?

What scenarios do you often imagine that cause you *irrational* worry?

What do you do to lessen your worry?

As you have grown older, do you worry more or less in general?

— 4 —

OVERCOME OFFENSES
AND INSULTS

He who is affected by an insult is infected by it.
—Jean Cocteau

DO YOU EVER FIND YOURSELF remembering times when you were insulted or offended by someone in a way that it shocked you so much that you were silent in response?

Or maybe you stuttered or stammered around and said something stupid in return and now, all this time later, you find yourself recalling those moments long gone and thinking of what you would have said or done if you had the chance to do it over again.

Isn't it amazing the power that words have? And the thoughts we have about those words. Negative or positive, the words uttered years ago can come back to haunt both the speaker and the listener depending on the situation.

In your daily life, it is a powerful skill to be able to quickly guide your thoughts past offense and insult in order to keep moving forward toward your goals. The longer you are able to stay present and on the edge of what is happening, the more clearly we will think. When we let our emotions get involved due to letting our feelings get hurt over careless words, our minds become cloudy and we stall our progress.

The second you feel the sting of insult is the trigger to push that thought out of your mind and come back to the moment immediately and move forward to the next moment.

FOUR STEPS FOR OVERCOMING OFFENSE

1. Don't take anything personal
2. Recognize when you're imagining someone else's ill-intentions and reject those thoughts
3. Don't feed or spread negative energy
4. Be present in the next moment

STICKS AND STONES

Live in the moment and those insults go in one ear and out the other, as they say. If you watch and listen to a group of childhood friends, especially in their teenage years, they will often pick on each other and trade barbs that border on mean or offensive, but minutes later they are all talking or playing as if none of it meant anything. Which in most cases, it did not.

This is not always true and, yes, words can hurt. Many young people have the problem of taking insults too personally or some of the insults can be so mean-spirited that they cause great damage to another person.

I'm not talking about those extreme situations but more of the everyday workplace banter that is thoughtless and occasionally causes offense.

Don't give other people's words more power than they should have.

Don't give other people's words more power than they should have.

Why is it that sometimes as adults, our skin becomes thin

and we take words personally and give them much more power? Being present-minded is the antidote to mulling over perceived harsh or offensive words from others. Move right along to the next moment. There is no time to waste.

IT ALL STARTS WITH A THOUGHT

For the present, it is sufficient if you remember that you are living daily, in the midst of all manner of thought impulses which are reaching your subconscious mind, without your knowledge. Some of these impulses are negative, some are positive. You are now engaged in trying to help shut off the flow of negative impulses, and to aid in voluntarily influencing your subconscious mind, through positive impulses of DESIRE. When you achieve this, you will possess the key which unlocks the door to your subconscious mind. Moreover, you will control that door so completely, that no undesirable thought may influence your subconscious mind.

Everything which man creates, BEGINS in the form of a thought impulse. Man can create nothing which he does not first conceive in THOUGHT. Through the aid of the imagination, thought impulses may

be assembled into plans. The imagination, when under control, may be used for the creation of plans of purposes that lead to success in one's chosen occupation.
—Napoleon Hill, *Think and Grow Rich*

Everything beginning with a thought means the offense you take and the offense you give are controllable. When you take offense and react by insulting the other person or by being passive-aggressive, you have spread negative energy and have given up the power to control your perspective.

DO SOMETHING PHYSICAL TO COUNTERACT NEGATIVE THINKING

If you are having a hard time moving forward for whatever reason—maybe you are criticizing yourself for a failure or you are wrestling with resentment, doing something physical like taking a walk outside or doing calisthenic exercises can be the impetus to get you back on track.

Maybe the offense is big enough that you need to talk to the other person involved to work things out in order to move on.

Again, when you are paying attention to what is happening in the now, you will recognize the self-doubt or negative self-talk and be able to choose one of the many remedies for changing your attitude and actions. If you are living in the future or dwelling on the past, you do not have those options because you will not even recognize the real problem.

PERSONAL REFLECTIONS

Is there an offense or an insult that you are struggling to let go of?

Who in your life is mostly likely to cause you emotional pain and why?

In what ways can you let go of the pain of insult so that you can move quickly forward into the next moments of your life?

Think of a phrase or a quote that you can memorize and keep in your mind to remember the next time you are insulted.

Are there any situations in your life right now in which you should address someone regarding an insult or offense? Are you harboring resentment that you could let go of by discussing it with the person?

Do you tend to be critical of yourself for saying foolish things or for speaking up when you should have been silent?

What are some daily goals you could set for yourself to help you deal with insults and offenses from fellow humans?

— 5 —

SLOWING DOWN TIME

*Life moves pretty fast. If you don't stop and look
around once in a while, you could miss it.*
—Ferris Bueller

**When life is moving too fast, come back to the
present to slow down time.**

In the modern world in which everything seems
to be moving faster including cars, information,
technological developments, the building of
infrastructure; sometimes it feels like even the
passage of time itself seems to be sped up. Life
can often feel like a high-speed, frenzied race to
the finish line. As a result, you may find yourself in
moments of extreme stress. It may feel like the world
depends on the decision you make, or that the walls
of your life are closing in on you, or that there is no
time to even sleep.

When you notice the level of mental stress heighten to points like those I have described, try the following exercise:

Take a deep breath, breathe out slowly.

Say to yourself, "here and now."

Do this a few times in a row until your body begins to calm down and your mind follows.

Of course, we still must think about the future. The way we imagine or dream of our destiny, it all happens in the present moment, but it is important because our vision determines how we react to the moments that happen next.

A person who cannot imagine the future is a person who cannot contemplate the results of his actions. Some are thus paralyzed into inaction.
—Alan Lightman, *Einstein's Dreams*

Everything we do now will have consequences tomorrow even though we are fully appreciating the fact that today is all we know for certain. So in living in the present, we plan for the future.

Every action you prepare to take, think about it for a couple seconds.

IS IT NECESSARY TO DO OR SAY THIS?

Being present-minded helps us to catch ourselves before saying things unnecessarily, especially complaints or negative comments. For example, I wanted to complain to my wife about not canceling my dentist appointment this morning after we had talked about it the day before. I was busy at work and did not want to go. So I thought about texting her to say something like "...wish we would've canceled the appointment." She was also at work and my text might have added to the stress that she was already dealing with at her job, and it would have been a useless piece of communication.

So I caught myself and did not text her and went to the appointment. The other alternative is that I could have called to cancel the appointment myself which would have been the productive response if I had decided not to go. The point is, especially with someone like our spouse, it is easy to say negative things in passing, to complain and think nothing of it. But when we do this, we are putting more stress into the universe and causing anxious energy around us.

It seems like a little thing to refrain from saying or texting something negative, but it prevents the ripple effect of pessimistic thoughts from affecting others.

Ask yourself at every moment, is this necessary.
—Marcus Aurelius

This idea of slowing down time and influencing positive thoughts and energy also applies to your personal development goals. It affects every aspect of your growth.

FOUR METHODS FOR SLOWING DOWN TIME

1. Observe in detail something in your immediate surroundings
2. Be present and listen to the words, voices, and sounds around you

3. Refrain from unnecessary negative communication
4. Wake up early and spend time alone reflecting on your thoughts

Whether you are at work, at the gym, at church, at the movies, or at home, be conscious and mindful of your situation and the moments you are experiencing rather than thinking of what you need to do at the other places.

BE WHERE YOU ARE

When you are on vacation, are you often thinking about what needs to be done when you get home or back to work? Are you thinking about the trip back home when you are still on the beach?

Work on making a conscious effort to be aware that you are not back home yet, you are on vacation. Try to place yourself in the moment and space you are in. There can be a pressure to enjoy yourself or to "have fun" to the point where it feels forced, but that is not what I am suggesting. The point is to be able to come back to the present in your mind so that you are not thinking about events that have not happened yet.

At some point, yes, you have to think about future events that are planned for when you return home from vacation, but you do not have to think about them beyond what needs to be done preparation-wise, and you do not need to continue thinking about these things all the time. Being present wherever you are slows down time.

There is so much peace in just letting go and being present in each moment while not thinking of anything other than what you are doing. When you can stop seeking more, if only for that second, you can experience infinite contentment.

Being present wherever you are slows down time.

A challenge: Today let your thoughts arise and pass and stay conscious, exercise your will in all hours and make progress. Stay in the mix, talk to people, and make your life more pleasurable and tolerable by being proactively involved in creating the environment for your mind to be healthier.

PERSONAL REFLECTIONS

Think about slowing down time. Do you ever wish time would slow down? What do you notice about your environment when you have thoughts like this?

What are you doing when time seems to disappear?

How often do you pause before saying something or texting?

Does the stress in your life cause the days to go by too fast? Or maybe not fast enough?

Think about your perspective when things are stressful. Is there a way to put a positive spin on the stressors?

Do you tend to think of what needs to be done next when you should be enjoying the moment? Think of some times when you are inclined to do this and make it a goal to be more present in those situations.

What are some ways you can practice calming your mind down when your thoughts begin to get hectic?

— 6 —

STAY BUSY, CONTROL EMOTIONS

In times of great stress or adversity, it's always best to keep busy, to plow your anger and your energy into something positive.
—Lee Iacocca

FOCUS AND FOLLOW what your mind tells you to do to build you, help you, fuel your creativity, push you forward toward your goals. When you are stressed, run to something positive, not negative.

For example, I am sitting here overwhelmed with decisions to make and tasks to complete by certain deadlines. I would sit here and overthink everything and do nothing, but my mind tells me to get down on the floor and do some push-ups. And I know this will build me even if only my body. So I get down on the floor and do push-ups and I feel better.

Of course, when you are driving down the road, it won't be practical to stop and do some push-ups and your mind is not likely going to suggest such a thing. But it might tell you to turn on some music when you are thinking too much about a problem or anticipated event. Your conscience may remind you to be grateful.

Your conscience may suggest thinking of all of it from an entirely different angle. These hints from your mind—if they are life giving, then they are worth paying attention to and following out.

Stay busy to forget emotions that don't serve you. Emotions like boredom, depression, anger, resentment, shame, and embarrassment. Get over your emotions by getting busy exercising, and doing housework that needs to be done. Do some cooking that needs to be done. Do some repair projects, building projects, or creative projects like photography, writing, and film.

Get back into the moment by doing something physical.

All of this insight can only come to you if you are existing fully in the present moment. Otherwise, you will revert to your habits. What do I mean by fully? I mean not checking your phone or thinking about the time, thinking about what to have for your next meal, or anything else that will come to mind. All the distractions of life that require so much time are sometimes opportunities to practice being present mindful, but they can also be things that are meant only to cause distraction to the one thing that you were already doing and that thing usually is a creative endeavor.

Get back into the moment by doing something physical.

FOUR WAYS TO REMOVE EMOTION AND BE PRODUCTIVE

1. Channel anger and frustration into your exercise
2. Listen to music while you work if possible
3. Stay away from the daily news
4. Remember that change is constant

When you are fully present in those moments *that you don't recognize as moments*, but only as the thing you are doing, then you are existing entirely—mind and body—in the present moment.

The external circumstances of the moment changes. The things you are doing in the moment obviously are changing as well—not every moment of course—but over time as a consideration. Over the course of a day for example. But why?

Because your mind tells you something else needs to be done. You need to get something to eat; you have to go to the bathroom, or you need to go to bed, etc. It tells you to reach over and take a drink even subconsciously. So much of our life is programmed, so what this really is is a battle for control over the mind. And it is and always will be a struggle due to our lack of understanding of the full use of our brains.

Every day, be prepared to make choices in the moment that align with your goals.

PERSONAL REFLECTIONS

What do you do each morning to prepare for the day's battle for the mind?

How can you remind yourself today that you have a choice each moment?

What is your go-to activity (positive or negative) when you feel stressed or frustrated?

If you turn to destructive choices when you are stressed, what are some choices you could make instead that would build you up and move you in a forward direction toward your goal?

What can you think of to motivate yourself to improve your daily choices starting tomorrow?

— 7 —

ALIGN WITH YOUR BIGGEST GOALS TODAY

You will become as small as your controlling desire;
as great as your dominant aspiration.
—James Allen

WE ARE SLOWED DOWN by thoughts that tell us "someday" will be better than today, better than right now. But in reality, there is no other time than now. So dig into whatever it is that you want to do, and even if "dig in" means to begin writing down some ideas about what you envision, then so be it. Go for it... today!

It is action that makes the emotions flow. Energizing the brain into thinking of ideas and then writing them down begins to crystallize those ideas into goals and realistic visions of success. And this is how you use the present moment to get something done toward your highest goal.

What is your most ambitious goal again? What is your dream life? Write it down once again or repeat it to yourself here and now. Doing this is another way of using the present moment to strengthen your resolve and to make the images of your dreams more clear and detailed and foremost in your thoughts.

Do not make the mistake of sacrificing time on your dreams by focusing on a notion of a future start date or time to begin working on them. Speaking of work, work is another way of staying in the present moment for extended periods of time. You have to work to make anything happen. You have to get lost in the work and let it pull you along so that you no longer are hampered by time.

Working is the fastest way to create change in your life.

The more you can sink into your work and find time to digest the thoughts that you have about your goals, the higher your chances of success in accomplishing your goals. I guess that sounds obvious, but it is one of the things that I overlook because it is so obvious.

It is something that is hidden in plain sight so to speak.

What can you do right now, right this second? For some people, reading this book is an effort toward their goal. How?

Achieving the right mindset is critical when it comes to creating a different life for yourself. To realize your dreams, you have to consistently check your perspective and do the work required to change it when it is negative. Daily, hourly, sometimes moment to moment. Help keep your perspective in check by monitoring your information intake.

Working is the fastest way to create change in your life.

CONSUMING POSITIVE INFORMATION

Do you know anyone who watches the news regularly, almost as entertainment? What are their attitudes like? I am thinking of a guy who consumes the news and political content every day, and he is pessimistic and often fearful about the future. Of course, there are reasons to stay informed and know about some of what is happening in the world at large (although one could argue it is more important to be concerned about local events that actually influence your life on a daily basis). When you worry about what is happening on the other side of the country or the world or if you are upset about what one politician says and what another political party is doing, then you give your energy to something you likely cannot control.

You are wasting the time you could be spending enjoying the moment. Not only that, you are likely affecting your perspective on the day in a negative way.

SEE THE RICHNESS OF BEING ALIVE

There is beauty all around you. Turn off the news, close your internet browser, and be careful of what you are reading on social media platforms. There is a choice in what you consume and how you spend your time. The choices you make influence your perspective and your overall mood and attitude. Once again, keeping a proper perspective is critical in making daily progress toward your goals.

So think through this carefully and decide whether it might be time to bow out of the political conversation for a while. Evaluate yourself and consider whether your negative mood of late might be caused by what you have been consuming news-wise and entertainment-wise.

Your entertainment is important too. Make sure what you do for entertainment does not drain your energy or saddle you with negative thoughts. All of these little things turn out not to be so little at all. "Little" things like what you read and watch determine so much of how you feel. "Little" things like what you choose to eat and whether or not you choose to exercise, all of these add up to the possibilities or lack thereof of realizing your dreams. The possibilities of change or stagnancy. The likelihood of your becoming who you want to be hinges on all these mundane choices we have to make each day.

Once again, each moment we have a choice.

CONSIDER YOUR CHOICES

Every thought that comes into your mind can be pushed aside or dwelled upon and concentrated on and turned into something bigger and more influential. Each thought can be cast aside as well. You may have ignored a certain thought many different times throughout your day. Stay strong.

The flip side is that the positive thoughts can be ignored as well. Pay attention to why you might not want to follow out your positive thoughts. What if you have a thought about a certain task that you could get done over your lunch break at work? Do you make an excuse to not do it and instead think of something else to do? Or do you make the effort to get that task done over lunch and feel good about crossing it off your list?

What about lunch choices? Do you have the thought of bringing a healthy lunch that you prepared at home? Or do you push that thought aside and head over to the fast food restaurant nearby where you work?

Our reactions to these types of thoughts can tell us a lot about our current attitudes and perspectives. And then we can tweak our perspectives and attitudes accordingly based on what is going on in our lives at the moment. Our perspectives can be changed gradually without our realizing it and sometimes we need to check ourselves through intentionally observing which thoughts we are giving our attention to and why.

Learn and grow from your thoughts and actions.

LIVE IN ALIGNMENT

Keep in the forefront of your mind that person who you want to become and live according to how that person would live. Make the choices that person would make. You are becoming this person through the decisions you make and the actions you take. So make decisions that the best version of yourself—the person you wish to become—would make so that you begin to morph and meld into that character.

Before you know it, the actual you will be indistinguishable from the ideal you have for yourself.

PERSONAL REFLECTIONS

Are your daily choices in line with your biggest goals?

What is your highest priority when it comes to your goals in life?

How do small choices you make impact your perspective and mood throughout the day?

What can you do today to bring you closer to your biggest goals?

What can you do today to keep your energy high and your perspective positive?

Are there entertainment and social media feeds that you might do better without? Think about the various forms of information you consume daily.

What choices did you make yesterday that you can consider and learn something from today? Based on your answer, what could you do differently today or tomorrow?

— 8 —

MINIMIZING DISTRACTIONS

Always hold fast to the present hour.
Every state of duration, every second,
is of infinite value...
—Goethe

OUR THOUGHTS ARE UNPREDICTABLE and given to change quickly.

For example, the fickleness of our mind is such that it can be derailed by reading an article or a blog post. Just this morning while I was writing, someone I love and respect texted me a link to a news article with a terrific click-bait title. I responded to the alert of my phone and then to the text itself and then clicked on the link. After reading the fascinating article, I began to read some of the 237 comments below.

Suddenly, I was pulled into differing opinions and other articles and studies being cited and political bents and conspiratorial outlooks, and on and on. By the time I was done reading that short article, an hour and a half had gone by. I found myself depressed and maybe a little angry inside from processing the words and ideas I had just consumed. I questioned how much of what I read was true, and what it all meant, and what I could do about any of it.

My writing had stopped and my attention had been hijacked by a simple text with an article I did not need to read.

This example of distraction illustrates the importance of minimizing possible distractions before beginning your work, and it also illustrates the chain reaction of our behaviors in our daily existence.

Imagine I did not answer the text. Nothing would have been hurt by waiting to look at that text much later in the day and then deciding whether to read the linked article or not. But because I responded almost unconsciously and immediately to my phone's alert, I lost hours of writing and had my attitude and mood changed for the worse.

THREE KEYS TO REDUCING DISTRACTION

1. Put your phone in another room when working if possible
2. Be prepared to be tempted by distractions when you begin to work
3. Eliminate or cut back on pleasurable bad habits

Remember, the goal is to "hold fast to the present hour." The value of the moment can only be appreciated if we stay there long enough to experience it fully. When we start thinking about cravings or what would make this moment even better, that's when the trouble starts. Distractions are easily accepted once we begin seeking more from the moment.

One common form of addiction and interruption in our lives comes with our phones that we carry with us everywhere. Social media.

SOCIAL MEDIA BARRAGE

Continue to avoid social media traps set for maximum distraction via comments and disagreements and political hot button issues that cause division, labels, and broad stroke generalizations.

Stay focused on the light, not the darkness and get your work done daily. You will not accomplish anything if you are worried about the future and the numerous things that could go wrong but probably will not.

What do you need to do next to move forward?

Once you begin filtering your content intake, a strange thing will begin to happen. You will see the world in a more positive light, and by the world, I mean people and incidental events throughout the day. You will find that you do not get as angry when someone cuts you off in traffic for example. Or when someone is rude to you at the grocery store, or in an email message. You realize that their rudeness is a reflection of what is going on in their life and has nothing to do with you at all and you forgive them and move along.

Without the constant onslaught of fear and loathing, you will begin to see the beauty in nature more frequently and laugh at jokes and your silly sense of self-importance.

When you start to lessen the negative and alarming influences, you start to better focus on and understand the essence of living in the moment. Focus on today and let tomorrow's troubles come as they may. Prepare your mind and face the day. The transformation you will experience over time will surprise and delight you.

Prepare your mind and face the day.

CULTURE OF FEAR
(distraction from the present)

Part of your transformation will be a disposal of vices. Your anxiety and neurotic habits of using vices to help you feel better will go away as you look less into the future and stay more in the minute-by-minute existence.

The seconds of our lives make up more than the hours of our lives in a lot of ways. The habitual anticipatory outlook of a driven society, an ambitious society, a culture that tells us that the most important thing is to be productive and successful, and that the production will lead to a better and better future while at the same time, that culture churns out endless stories of horrible violence and corruption among people, nations, politicians and corporations... this noise, this rumbling in the background of our days conditions us to be fearful. The fear causes us to look too far ahead and speculate too much which in turn causes us to miss the beauty of the moments we are experiencing.

It all adds up to distraction.

Looking ahead causes us to miss out on the peacefulness of the here and now. Being prepared is different than being anxious, you can prepare with an awareness of this moment.

Remember, the experience of doing whatever it is you are doing right now contains the miracle of being alive.

DROP THE VICES

Back to vices, we use them to escape the moment oftentimes. If you have any habits you would like to get rid of, here is a strategy for you. Notice when you go to them, whether it is food or drugs or whatever, any habits that get in the way of what you want to accomplish or that negatively impact your health—can you pay close attention to your thoughts the next time you reach for it?

The next time today or tomorrow that you begin to act out the offending habit, notice what is on your mind surrounding that vice. What are your exact thoughts as you pour that wine or light up the cigarette or drive to grab that burger and fries or pick up that cheesecake or... okay, you get the point.

How would you characterize your thoughts in those moments? Negative or positive? Stressed or excited? If your thoughts are telling you that you should not do what you are about to do, and you ignore them and go ahead and do it anyway, what thoughts do you have to rationalize this avoidance or dismissal of your conscience?

It would be interesting to write those thoughts down immediately. Read them, turn them around in your mind and examine them. You might find that they contain some keys that might help you overcome your base desires—your habits that you have made so strong by repeatedly ignoring your own good advice to yourself.

You may even find within those words the source of the pain which could be the trigger that caused you to reach for the vice in the first place many years ago.

And this is just one of the many ways living in the present moment can benefit you down the road. If you are able to find victory over long-held negative habits just by paying attention to the here and now, think about how much you could accomplish and bring to fruition if you are able to stay in that present mental state for extended lengths of time. Periods of uninterrupted creativity and productivity would become the norm, and you would not make excuses because you would not have the time for them.

Bad habits end up as costly distractions.

Work on dropping those vices by not giving in to your excuses in the seconds when they enter your mind.

PERSONAL REFLECTIONS

What are your most frequent distractions?

Think about why you might tend to click on trending searches on the internet. Why do we get caught up in stories served to us that have nothing to do with us?

What interruptions to your work do you often experience?

Describe your cell phone use. Are there any times throughout the day when you work that you could turn it off?

What kind of news and information causes you to be worrisome or fearful in your attitude?

Think of ways to replace fearful outlooks with optimistic views without being unrealistic.

What are three ways you can focus on your work more?

What is one habit you would like to drop in order to spend more time achieving your goals?

What is a positive habit you could implement to replace a current bad habit?

— 9 —

MANIFEST YOUR FUTURE

Ask for what you want and be prepared to get it.
—Maya Angelou

MINDFULNESS CAN BE USED as therapy, and it can also be used for revelation. Sit with yourself in perfect silence and let the imagery of your desired future come into your mind. Who is it that you want to be? What kind of influence do you wish to have? In what ways would you help others if you were this person?

Picture all of what comes to mind in response to these questions.This vision is your calling. It is your responsibility to follow it out and bring every detail to fruition. Let go of the years of fear and self-doubt just for right now. Practice letting go of all negative opinions of self and external concerns each morning.

You are ready today to begin following your call. There is no time for procrastination. Rest confident in the truth that today is all you have. This moment is forever. Begin living your future according to what manifests in your mind. Your burning desire is your purpose. Create that vision by the way you live and the choices you make each day.

Self-doubt and negative self-talk is ingratitude and unkindness. Do whatever it takes to dispel the feelings of darkness that daily will threaten to derail you and disrupt you from attaining the self-improvement and growth necessary to reach the full potential of your life. It will take perseverance, focus, and mindfulness to overcome the obstacles of negative energy that you will encounter on your journey to manifesting the future through living in the present.

To the being fully alive, the future is not ominous but a promise; it surrounds the present like a halo.

—John Dewey

Remove from your mind the temptation to go along with and be part of the status quo energy of this world. Prepare for greatness instead. Comfort and familiarity seems like the easy route, but the regret will not be easy when it comes.

Do not fear the power you have within. Do not fear the power you have to create lasting change, impact, and improvement in this world. Dare to be different. Share what you have learned with the world.

Keep on trying, doing your best to walk in the calling of the miracle of your life.

Motivate, create, and don't hate yourself or other people.

Manifest your future in the presence of God and humanity. We are all on our phones and still missing the call. Put your phone down and find some place to be silent. Listen. Close your eyes if needed. Release the need to find something to do to pass the time.

Your future will become clear to you. What is stuck in your mind in these times of mindfulness that says something to you about who you are and who you are to become? Write it down if you can. Listen to that persistent voice in the back of your mind.

What can you do about it right now? Do you need to write down an idea or ten? Make a phone call or a decision that you have been wavering on?

Try to work uninterrupted and see where your work takes you. What is revealed through your efforts?

Do you really want to be doing what you are currently doing?

Practice asking yourself questions and implementing silent meditations like these to help you see where you are and where to go from here.

INSIGHTS AND IDEAS

Get those insights, descriptions, and ideas about your future poured out of your mind and into your notebook. Force yourself to take 10 minutes and just dump ideas from your mind onto the page. Push yourself.

Do the work and find the answers in the work. The truth you seek is in the action you take. Are you still messing around when you should be focused? Are you really going to pursue the future you have manifested or are you just talking?

Right now, you are in the place where you can level up and get closer to who you want to be if you put in the work to become disciplined. Follow the guiding light of your spirit.

The truth you seek is in the action you take.

PERSONAL REFLECTIONS

Describe the vision you have. Do you understand that the work to become the person you envision is your purpose?

What part of your vision do you have self-doubt about?

What part of your vision of your future self do you feel confident about?

How can you begin to live in the way your future self would live right now?

What areas of your vision require the most work?

Think of a line to repeat to yourself the next time you feel tempted to give up on your calling and stay where you are in life.

Imagine the regret you will feel later in life if you do not give all you can to become what you should be.

— 10 —

ORGANIZED AWARENESS

For every minute spent organizing, an hour is earned.
—Ben Franklin

PART OF LIVING in the present is being aware of your surroundings and keeping the affairs of your life organized and ready.

Organizing and preparing (prepping) for difficult times, gaining financial stability through frugalness and investment, cleaning your house, office, and car—all of these are important steps to your success in life whatever your goal, and these are actions that build habits.

Author and psychologist Jordan Peterson made a strong point when he said something along the lines of "if you want to fix society, start by cleaning your room." He goes further to say, start with making your bed. The idea behind this now popular sound-bite is that there are a lot of people trying to change the world who have not changed themselves in the areas where they know that they should. They do not have their own life together, yet they are giving advice to others on a large scale or have ambitions of changing the economy, etc.

The point Peterson makes is that when we come back to our immediate part of life and living on a daily basis, we start with waking up in the morning and establishing the organizational habit of making our bed. Perhaps from there, it is cleaning our room and keeping it neat and organized. These tasks may seem inconsequential, but the psychological effect they have on us is significant.

Progress is made when we focus on what we can fix today in our own lives.

We begin to build confidence and competence and achieve bigger and better things through our preparation in the present moment, in the space that we occupy now.

Little things influence the big things. The tasks you complete today and the decisions you make each moment are what make up your tomorrow.

Progress is made when we focus on what we can fix today in our own lives.

PAY ATTENTION

By living in the moment, you can drastically reduce the time you waste in self-conscious behavior and thinking that causes you to feel anxious thoughts and consequently miss out on the enjoyment of the event you are experiencing. Even if it is not an enjoyable event to begin with, when you are constantly thinking about how you are appearing to others and what they are thinking of you, then you are missing opportunities to learn from what you are experiencing.

To lessen this kind of overthinking, the first thing you can do is pay attention. By paying attention as thoroughly as possible to what is happening now, you will focus your attention outward rather than inward on yourself. When you focus on others, you naturally will not spend as much time worrying about what they are thinking of you. As is often noted, most people will agree that this is a struggle (being self-conscious), and they are likely as worried about what you think of them as you are of them.

Paying attention to the task and moment at hand is confident behavior, and not only that, it increases your creative thought processes.

CREATIVITY BOOST

Try it for yourself. We miss the forest for the trees as they say, yes, but we also miss the trees for the forest and that can be quite enough to derail us or tempt us to want to quit.

> *One step at a time is all it takes to get there.*
> —Emily Dickinson

Look around you and see the opportunity. It is there if you will pause and breathe and pay attention to the details of your existence. It is there, there is truth and beauty and originality and creativity and productivity all waiting for you, waiting to be harvested and used to help create a better version of yourself and the future you have imagined.

The amount of inspiration we walk by, drive by, and frankly, ignore, on a daily basis could be the basis for your new company. It could form the outline of your new book. The missed signs could point straight to the business opportunity you have been desperately hoping and searching for.

Take your time.

Find your diamonds and gold in the mines that surround you. Appreciate the experience of the daily routine, of the miracle of your existence and the witness you bear to all that is wonderful, kind, and life giving.

PERSONAL REFLECTIONS

How often do you think about other things when you should be concentrating on your work?

What causes you to daydream? Can you think of some personal motivators to help yourself come back to the present each time you start to drift off in your mind?

If you are bored with your work, is it time for a change or is there a way to concentrate despite feelings of boredom?

What areas of your life could improve with organization?

What situations cause you to worry about what other people are thinking of you? If you could eliminate the time spent in this anxious state of mind, how much additional time would you have to be working on other things?

— 11 —

CONFIDENCE THROUGH MINDFULNESS

Nothing so bolsters our self-confidence and reconciles us with ourselves as the continuous ability to create; to see things grow and develop under our hand, day in, day out.
—Eric Hoffer

CONFIDENCE IS SOMETHING you were born with...or not. Right? It's luck.

Of course, people can "work" on it and practice "being confident" and then eventually over time, they could improve their confidence...but only to an extent. I mean, the people I knew who I would describe as confident were more outgoing and confident all of their lives. Even as children, they were enthusiastic and energetic around other people, while other kids were quiet and more inclined to follow than lead.

There is truth to that characterization. Some people are more on the extroverted side while others are more introverted. But consider the idea of confidence in a different way.

What if confidence wasn't a quality or human characteristic to be born with or without, but instead was a simple description of behavior?

Bestselling author Augusten Burroughs writes the following in his book, *This is How*:

Confidence is not something you feel or possess; it's something others use to describe what they see when they look at you. The experience others call confidence you experience as being fully at ease, fully yourself, and not self-conscious but rather task conscious.

As long as you pay attention only to what is happening right here, right this instant, you will be more fully yourself... It's a byproduct of focus.

Also, focus is a byproduct of being in the present moment. Focus and confidence come from being immersed in the now.

So thinking about Burroughs' words, the confidence we seek is not to be found if we imagine it primarily as a word used to describe human behavior. Focus on being present in your work instead. Your actions will then manifest as confidence. When you stay in the moment, you forget about yourself and how you appear.

Focus on being present in your work and your actions will manifest as confidence.

Speaking of manifesting confidence, take a minute or two to consider the powerful process described below.

NAPOLEON HILL'S SELF-CONFIDENCE FORMULA

One of the steps in Napoleon Hill's formula for self-confidence is to write down and repeat the following words to yourself:

I realize the dominating thoughts of my mind will eventually reproduce themselves in outward, physical action, and gradually transform themselves into physical reality, therefore, I will concentrate my thoughts for thirty minutes daily, upon the task of thinking of the person I intend to become, thereby creating in my mind a clear mental picture of that person.

Do this little exercise daily even if you can only do it for five minutes, and you will begin to be so focused on the work of becoming who you want to be that you will begin to think far less of what other's opinions of you might be. It is a gradual process that leads to confidence as you achieve your goals one at a time, one day at a time. Always keep in mind the person you want to become, how you'll look, the amount of money you have, your family relationships and other parts of your life that you can envision.

It works especially well to recite this mantra just before you go to sleep at night.

CHANGE YOUR MOTIVATION

If you have kids, you go after success because you want them to be proud of you and follow in your footsteps and be proud of themselves. You want them to want to be like you, not just tolerate you.

Reach your goals for the people around you at work, the people that come into contact with you. Show up and be consistent with your words so you can help other people and guide them.

You work out for them, you drop all your vices for them, and you go after material and spiritual growth for them.

Stop making excuses for *yourself*. No, you don't get to drink a six-pack or a bottle of wine tonight just because you had a hard day at work. No, you don't get to order pizza for dinner just because you worked late and failed to prepare a healthy meal.

Start with your loved ones and become better for them, and then you will find yourself and how you can help others. Then you will find the success and the things that have eluded your efforts thus far. It is time to change your source of motivation.

You will become more and more confident as you consistently accomplish goals every day eventually achieving what you once only dreamed of.

THREE STEPS TO CONFIDENCE

How to be confident about what you are doing—remember these 3 things:

1. Work on your goals relentlessly.

Which leads to not paying so much attention to what others think.

Which leads to people describing you as confident, because you are doing what you should be doing instead of worrying about anything else.

2. Spend time every day envisioning the person you wish to become while doing and creating in alignment with your vision.

3. Think of someone else who will be helped by you achieving your goals. Do it for them and be relentless.

THE REAL YOU

Being present makes you more authentic. You are closer to the true nature of yourself when you are existing fully in the moment, and others will notice this as well. You will become more attractive through this authenticity as people like to be around people who are real and not phony.

Authenticity is the beginning of your magnetism and pleasing personality that will help you to be social and increase your network. You will be able to relate to people more, ask better questions, and listen more carefully when you are present.

Every moment is a choice, a minute in time where you can make a decision to take positive action or to continue dwelling on a negative thought. Each choice made in those moments compounds your present perspective and attitude.

PERSONAL REFLECTIONS

Who are some people in your life who you would describe as confident, and why would you say so?

What about you? Do you consider yourself to be confident? Why or why not?

What activities do you participate in that make you forget what other people think about you?

What do you want to create?

Who do you love? Can you envision yourself becoming a better person for them?

In what ways would a better version of you be a better friend, partner, brother, sister, mother or father?

— 12 —

PRESENT-MINDED PATIENCE

Patience is necessary, and one cannot reap
immediately where one has sown.
—Soren Kierkegaard

DEVELOPING AND MAINTAINING patience with yourself and with others is an awesome byproduct of living in mindfulness each day.

Mindfulness builds patience.

We are in a battle with an instant-gratification, consumerism-based culture to accept that what we are becoming will take time. If you are constantly looking for the big results instead of the accomplishments of the little, daily goals, you will eventually become discouraged. You might even quit. It is all about establishing your day-to-day program and staying present within it to build yourself.

Mindfulness builds patience.

The more present you are, the more patient you can become. The more patient you become, the higher your stress management possibilities are. The more stress you can handle, the higher your potential in business. So one piece of personal development affects another.

To work on being more patient and mindful start with the mundane activities of the day.

NO HURRY

Do you find yourself rushing through simple tasks like getting dressed or eating a meal? What about stopping at the grocery store to pick up a couple items? There are many times I find myself hurrying through activities without a real need to do so. It might be just to get home sooner or to do the next thing. But if you are thinking about the weekend or the next task or the next event, you are projecting yourself into the future at the cost of not being present.

A "self-contained" man is never in a hurry; and a self-contained man keeps or contains his thought, his spirit, his power, mostly on the act or use he is making

at the present moment with the instrument his spirit uses, his body; and the habitually self-possessed woman will be graceful in every movement, for the reason that her spirit has complete possession and command of its tool, the body; and is not a mile or ten miles away from that body in thought, and fretting or hurrying or dwelling on something at that distance from her body.
—Prentice Mulford, *Thoughts are Things*

Become self-possessed by being calm and intentional in your actions. Being patient will help you focus longer and more intensely on the work that will get you closer to your goals.

QUALITY MATTERS

When you are fully engaged and concentrated on the activity you are undertaking, you can do it with excellence. Even something as simple as folding your clothes. Next time you fold laundry, pay attention to each movement of your hands and arms and watch each step of the process. You will find when your entire focus is on what you are doing, you naturally take extra care to do it well.

It doesn't mean you will do the work more slowly either. Actually, your speed of completing whatever you are doing might increase as your physical and mental activities tend to be more efficient when they are concentrated.

Increase the quality of your work by being present.

Your mind is not on other things, only the details of the task at hand.

Increase the quality of your work by being present.

YOU KNOW YOU CAN DO IT

Practice believing you can do what needs to be done even if it is not right away. We can create the life we are imagining, but it will require the patience to play the long game instead of looking for fast results.

A key to the game is the mental conditioning of imagining doing difficult things, and then coming to the realization that we can do hard things, then repeating that fact internally: *I can do difficult things.*

Start reprogramming your thoughts and soon you will change your beliefs. The next time you attempt and successfully complete a difficult undertaking, the end of your self-defeating disbelief will be near. You're building new ideas and confidence in yourself.

When the next challenge presents itself, the overwhelming feelings will not be so strong. They may still be there, but they won't have the power to stop you from taking action.

Thoughts of what's impossible won't control your life when you live in the moment and experience all of what *is* possible.

STAY PRESENT WITH THE PAIN

When we face a task that seems insurmountable or like an enormous, unmanageable amount of work— we begin to get outside of that moment, the moment where we should be imagining our victory and success in doing whatever the task is. Instead we grow impatient and we fall out of that groove and begin to let thoughts of the impossible, of the difficult, of the discouraging nature of life overtake us and cause us to procrastinate or complain or worry.

Then, of course, nothing gets done and the goal remains unfulfilled. Our mind believes that it is in fact impossible. This belief is without solid evidence in most cases, it's just our own thoughts and possibly the opinions of the others to whom we complained or pessimistically presented our goal/task/responsibility.

One step at a time and living in the moment is the way to emerge victorious over the trials and obstacles that seem insurmountable when taken as a whole. If we can maintain a state of mind that defaults to the moment and the smallest detail of a task, there is nothing we cannot overcome. Sink into to your work—whatever it is—and fixate and fascinate on the minutiae for as long as you can.

Watch as you wake up into a world where you accomplish a great deal without even realizing the time passing.

SLEEP BETTER

Speaking of waking up, patience and persistence leads to better rest at night which is incredibly helpful to your mind and body and allows you to wake up early, which is another hack for creating motivation for the day's goals. If you can start getting up an hour earlier in the morning, just five days a week, you give yourself 20 more hours per month to work on your goals. Going to sleep a little earlier and getting up a little earlier can buy you that prime productivity time in the morning.

You won't regret it once you have gotten up and begin to get some work done. After you do it for a few weeks in a row, you'll be loving the amount of work you get done and how waking up early simply becomes the way you live.

Early to bed and early to rise, makes you a more present-minded, patient person.

FIVE POWER-PACKED BENEFITS TO BECOMING PATIENT

1. You become more focused.
2. You can handle more stress.
3. You become more productive.
4. You become more confident.
5. You sleep better at night

PERSONAL REFLECTIONS

Do you rush or hurry through the mundane activities of your day?

Do you feel like you do not reach your goals quickly enough to stay motivated?

What limiting beliefs do you know that you have?

What goals do you have that make you feel overwhelmed when you get into the details of doing of them?

Do you tend to look for results too quickly? What are some ways you can relax into the present moment of each task on your list and develop the patience to accomplish them?

— 13 —

EXERCISE:
THE MIND-MUSCLE
CONNECTION

An early morning walk is a blessing for the whole day.
—Henry David Thoreau

SIMILAR TO THE PHYSICAL act of journaling in a note-book, exercising your muscles forces you to come into the present moment through action. Concentrating on the movements and contractions of your muscles while using your mind to push yourself beyond your limits allows you to transcend your distractions and worries and become stronger in the process.

You can change a negative mindset into a positive one through exercise. By intentionally moving your body out of the moment of dissatisfaction, you can leave that energy field and execute positive action that has long-term benefits for your body and short-term benefits for your mind.

CHANGE YOUR BELIEFS ABOUT EXERCISE

We have deceived ourselves into thinking that work and exercise are negative things and not to be desired when they are really the source of the pleasure we seek through other means. Program your mind through repetition to look forward to exercise and to only speak positively about it.

FIVE STEPS TO REPROGRAM YOUR ATTITUDE TOWARD EXERCISE

1. Exercise for a week, one day after another
2. Experience the benefits
3. Ride the momentum to exercise again today
4. Look forward to the good feelings of having exercised
5. Feel the regret when you miss it

When we stay in the habits of eating healthy food, exercising, and reflecting on positive material, we are excited to work toward our goals in a way we never thought was possible.

> *I know that creation is an intellectual and bodily discipline, a school of energy. I have never achieved anything in anarchy or physical slackness.*
>
> —Albert Camus

Once you experience the high of a good workout and the positive effects it has on your mind and body over time, you will begin to enjoy it. Then you will push yourself even further and begin to find comfort in the temporary discomfort of exercising your body contrary to what you previously believed. In this way, you will have changed your life through changing your beliefs.

It all starts with staying present with the pain and finding pleasure in the process of doing hard things.

BREAK DOWN THE PROCESS

Stay focused on the work today. Don't allow yourself to become depressed by entertaining pessimistic thoughts. One negative thought leads to another so as you become more present through patience and exercise, stop the negative thoughts right away by doing something positive.

The process of accomplishing what you want and becoming who you want to be is creating a ladder made up of small victories.

Be accountable to yourself and your goals. Commit yourself to pursuing and achieving the goals that will lead to the life you envision for yourself. *Follow your path and understand that present moment action that aligns with your vision creates future satisfaction and minimizes regret.*

In the moment, there is no impossible task. Breaking down the big picture into smaller snapshots is the way to become comfortable with imagining doing hard things. Experience meditation through physical exertion. Trust your workout.

Take a walk, lift some weights, go for a swim, or take a spin class for example, the possibilities for exercise are endless, just like the benefits. We tend to make life more complicated than necessary by staying introspective instead of taking some kind of physical action.

PERSONAL REFLECTIONS

Describe your perspective on exercise? Would you say it is a positive or negative outlook? Have you ever used physical activity to change your mental state?

Imagine being able to stay present with the pain. Are there certain parts of your goals and daily tasks that cause you pain? The next time it happens, experiment with staying present with the pain without running from it to persevere and finish the task you set out to complete.

What was your favorite form of exercise/sport/game as a child?

How can you incorporate physical activity into your daily routine, and how would it benefit you?

— 14 —

PREVENT REGRET, DISCOVER CONTENTMENT

*If you can be content right now, then you'll always
be content because it's always right now.*
—Willie Nelson

THE WAY TO REDUCE the potential for future guilt is to live the way you are being called to live right now. When you are doing what you should be doing each moment of the day, you will recognize contentment.

Live in alignment with your purpose and discover mental peace.

Contentment can be found in almost any circumstance, and being present allows you to be grateful for the day that you have, for the chance to live life right now and not hold back by counting on the future. Gratitude manifests itself as action.

And it feels good to put gratitude into the universe even for the small things. When you are preoccupied with the notorious "what I should have said or done" or with the fantasy of plans for the days ahead, you miss out on the potential of right now. Seize the opportunity of today.

Gratitude manifests itself as action.

Embrace the contradiction of not caring so much about what happens while finding beauty and meaning in the minor details of the moment.

Becoming the person you envision (your purpose in life) will give you the knowledge and healing necessary to be able to help others.

There is no downside to practicing mindfulness and being present daily. The benefits of living in the moment are numerous and our attitude and consequently our life will be greatly enhanced as we learn to live in a way that helps us focus, be grateful, and achieve our greatest potential.

Regret comes from not trying, from quitting and from ultimately selling ourselves short with limiting beliefs and escapism. When we do not follow our calling and instead, tell ourselves it is too hard, or it will take too long, or "I am not good enough," that is what causes immense regret. And the regret piles up and gets worse the longer we ignore our calling and the longer we wait to get our life in alignment with our purpose.

There is not a better time to start living in the present and transforming your life than right now. Start today and you will feel better tomorrow. No regrets, we have one life to live and share with others.

Of all the words of mice and men, the saddest are, "It might have been."
— Kurt Vonnegut

PERSONAL REFLECTIONS

Think about the things you regret in life already. Are they mostly things you've done, or the things you didn't do and no longer can?

What did you learn today?

Do you have a bucket list? What still remains on the list to be done?

What activities, places, or experiences bring you contentment?

What has helped you in your journey that you can share with others?

CONCLUSION

The best thing about the future is that
it comes one day at a time.
—Abraham Lincoln

BEING PRESENT IN the good moments but also in the bad ones: this is the key idea to making yourself believe in the power of the here and now.

Yourself being the idea you have of yourself, yes, but also the subconscious mind. Train your ego *and* subconscious mind to adopt new programming through repetition. And in the challenging moments, you find your true self and your current skill level. It's easy to be calm when life is good. As you begin to stay present when you are inconvenienced, when you are in pain, when you are angry, this is when you will be able to level up and gain more mind control.

For example, this morning I am:

Grateful to wake up and see another day.

Present in each experience.

Accepting what is.

The way to say yes to the instant is to accept it with all its beauty and ugliness. To appreciate the moment of being alive and acting and living in the way that you are right now. To find hope in the beauty and solace in the knowledge that the pain and sorrow will someday pass. To understand that life is both short and long and if you can live in the moment, it is eternity.

Learning from both the good and bad parts of human life and the labels we place on everything. Unlearning the labels we place on ourselves. To see life as a journey and a one-time experience, this perspective can help us appreciate our choices and the fact that our decisions do matter. We matter. Our lives impact others around us while we are alive and after we have died and passed on from this experience.

WHAT WE TALK ABOUT WHEN WE TALK ABOUT MINDFULNESS...

When we try to fully experience the present moment, we are talking about practice. It is an effort we make to loosen the hold our thoughts have over us, just for the moment. We are not trying to constantly be without thoughts. Instead, we are talking about a way of resetting the mind. We are pausing to let all that mental noise dissipate while we live physically in the space we are in.

As we gain skill in living in the present, the worry about ourselves lessens. We begin to simply act instead of think. Too much thinking is how all the self-doubt, self-judgment, and impulsive behavior flourishes.

When we stop thinking about ourselves, we are free to live positively, work on our goals, and be present and valuable to other people. But when we are in this obsessive mindstate focused on our worries, we are selfish and useless to others. We are neglecting our calling.

DEALING WITH PROBLEMS IN THE PRESENT

When you begin to improve, you will be tested. When you start working out and you stop drinking or overeating, right away, life's problems will come flying at you. Count on it. Maybe after a few days feeling proud of yourself and having high energy and productivity, you will be tested.

Family matters will arise and threaten to push you into an angry response. Let those feelings arise and pass until you can deal with the problems in a calm manner.

Financial burdens or worries will be laid on your shoulders, and you will be tempted to think negative thoughts as a result. Do not let thoughts and circumstances derail you. You have the strength and the power to continue to improve yourself and as you do, you will improve all areas of your life including family and finance.

And there's a good chance that it won't be just those areas that become a sudden source of stress and anxiety. There will be work problems, car problems, and problems due to weather. The point is, be prepared. Mentally, you can overcome these issues before and when you face them.

When you promise yourself to be present in the moment, it means the good moments, the moments where you are doing what you are called to do, and also the moments where life throws all manner of negativity at you and you have to figure out what to do with it. If you can stay present during the tough times, you will be in the best position to make good decisions about how to handle them.

Overcome those temptations to resort back to your vices during the hard times and you will become strong. Build the strength to overcome by remaining in the moment.

Be patient with yourself with your efforts to stay present with your current situation no matter what else is going on around you. Over time you will get better and better at this valuable skill.

Stay present while walking, running, lifting weights, writing, talking, listening, reading, texting, taking a shower, eating a meal, or taking out the trash. Stay present and notice how you calm down as the worry lessens and the anxious thoughts about the future fade away.

The power of staying present manifests as self-mastery in controlling the mind.

WE ARE ONE

It helps to understand that we are all chasing this idea of wholeness, completeness, or what some might call success. Our ideas of fulfillment vary. Our individual consciousness is fragmented into a mess of indecision, wild ambition, impulses, desires, emotions, and pain.

We progress by finding peace with what is happening now. By the understanding that all is what it is. We are not expecting a massive transformation to happen tomorrow. We are taking one moment at a time living with gratitude and appreciation for the experience and without expectation of comfort tomorrow. We are making good decisions and achieving small daily goals. We are connecting with people and understanding that they share all the fears, heartaches, and anxiousness that we do. We are them, and they are us and we are one.

One day at a time...focus on today and find satisfaction in getting the daily tasks done one more time. At night, you can lay your head down tired and at peace from living in line with your calling. Think about what you can improve upon tomorrow and wake up feeling great about developing into someone better than you were yesterday. Each day, one after another, show up and be committed to the path you have chosen.

CELEBRATE THE EXPERIENCE

I hope you find joy in the experience of taking life one day at a time, one moment at a time. We are not guaranteed tomorrow. This is not an excuse to not prepare for the future, but it is a reminder to enjoy the now! It is easy to get caught up in the worries of tomorrow at the expense of today and there is no good reason to do this.

EPILOGUE

Pleasure in the Present
By *Prentice Mulford*

Pleasure is the sure result of placing thought or force on the thing we are doing now, and pain of some sort in both present and future is the certain result of sending thought or force away from the act which needs to be done at this moment.

When we dress, eat, walk or do anything with mind placed on something else, we are making the present act irksome; we are training to make every act irksome and disagreeable; we are making the thing feared a certainty, for what we put out in thought as unpleasant is an actual thing, a reality. And the longer we continue to put it out the more force we add to it, and the more likely it is then to be realized in the physical world. To bring us what all want and are seeking for, namely—happiness, we need to have perfect control of our mind and thoughts at all times and places.

One most important and necessary means for gaining this, lies in this discipline regarding so-called little or trivial things, just as the discipline and movement of an army commences with the training of the private soldiers' legs and arms. If you hurry over these so-called petty details, you are easily thrown off guard or confused at unexpected occurrences, and in life it is the unexpected that is always happening.

> *In life, it is the unexpected that is always happening.*
>
> —Prentice Mulford

We need to always keep our mind present with us. We want it always on the spot ready to use in any direction. Our thoughts are not on the spot when we tie our shoes and think a mile from that shoe-string—when we sharpen a pencil and think of tomorrow's worries. Our mind is then away, and if it has for a lifetime been in the habit of straying from the act in hand to the act afar, it becomes more and more difficult to bring it back to use, and more difficult to use promptly when it is brought back. Our thoughts move from one thing to another with more than electric speed, and we can unconsciously train this quickness to be ever darting from one thing to another until it becomes almost impossible to keep it on one thing for ten consecutive seconds.

On the contrary, **through cultivation of repose and deliberation in all things, we can train ourselves to fasten our thoughts on anything as long as we please**, to throw ourselves into any mood of mind we please, and to throw ourselves at will into sleep or a semi-conscious, dreamy state as restful as sleep. These are very small parts of the possibilities for the human mind.

—Prentice Mulford, *Thoughts are Things*

ABOUT THE AUTHOR

John Martin shares years of experience and insights to help people analyze their mindset through introspection so they can eliminate whatever is suppressing their potential—and release whatever is begging to emerge. His goal is to motivate and free people to take action and persevere regardless of their current situation.

In addition to *Focus on Today* and his productivity books, John has also received acclaim for several other personal development books including *Choose Your Perspective* and *Empower Yourself.*

When he is not writing, he enjoys hanging out with his family, working with other authors on their books, reading, cooking, watching movies, and thinking about what he should be writing.

JOURNAL

_____

_____

_____

_____

_____

_____

_____

_____

_____

_____

_____

_____

_____

_____

_____

_____